T0095663

Buddings
Blossomings
Blessings

Patricia Kampmeier

InspiringVoices®

My thanks to the editors of the following publications,
in which some of these poems previously appeared:
poetry.com (These Perfect Things)

Cover Art: Watercolor Painting by Neva Lou Kampmeier

Scripture taken from the King James Version of the Bible.

Inspiring Voices books may be ordered
through booksellers or by contacting:

Inspiring Voices
1663 Liberty Drive
Bloomington, IN 47403
www.inspiringvoices.com
1 (866) 697-5313

ISBN: 978-1-4624-1206-8 (sc)
ISBN: 978-1-4624-1207-5 (e)

Print information available on the last page.

Inspiring Voices rev. date: 05/30/2018

CONTENTS

For those who have sung through me, thank you.

For my daughter, whose enthusiasm and encouragement have repeatedly lifted me.

For those who loved my first book, *I am Pat*, and told me so, thank you for telling me!

For my teachers, especially Mrs. Dorothy Lambert and Louise Yahnian, for what they taught and for their encouragement and appreciation. Further thanks to Charselle Hooper for letting me read at their monthly poetry gathering and to Dr. Clifford O. Adams, who was so supportive and appreciative of my poetry when I was a young woman, urging me to publish and opening a door for me at that time.

And again: "Let the words of my mouth, and the meditation of my heart, be acceptable in Thy sight, O Lord, my strength, and my redeemer." Psalm 19:14 (KJV)

It is my hope that you will read my book straight through from beginning to end, the first time.

PREFACE

These are poems flowing out from my senior, quiet, meditative self, yearning toward love and gratitude for life, for awareness, for people and animals, for almost all-that-is.

They move between inward and outward life, between joy and frustration, between clarity and confusion, between simplicity and complexity. I wonder about what is mine and what is not mine, as poems, like musical compositions, are often just given, arising in consciousness from somewhere and perhaps from someone, given in their entirety. I can only say thank you, again and again.

GIVING SELF

I said I would give you my life today in
    this new way
Of words and story-telling,
    rememberings and
Otherness. I am not free of my body yet.
Soon maybe I will be and then - who
    knows -
Maybe I still will give you my life this way
Or perhaps others will come inside
    with you
And give you of their lives, just as I
    am doing now.

We as people do not really understand
    with our
Minds but only with our intuitive
    hearts how this
Flow of consciousness between us
    brings forth
Words like these. May it be as a
    blessing to all
Of us as we grow into
Understanding of how this can be.

GOD GIVE ME THEN

God give me then whatever He gives
Until the new freshness of His rising
  life in me
Like sap's upthrust in trees and
Food and strength pushing upward in
  the plant and
Circulating blood and oxygen in my
  taut veins and arteries
And all upward-striving lifting uplifted
  pulsing
Into the gracious day of the sun's light
  and warmth
And ever ever increasing in
  joyousness and
Vitality all bursting forth in every
  which way
And God's life certainly and forever is

DELIGHT

Joy rushed through me
Bubbling up like fountains
Twirling and dancing
Felt like It was dancing
Delightedly through all my
Body's systems
So much energy
So much rising-upness and
Outwardness and
Beyondness
Maybe all my cells and molecules
Dancing with delight
And the Light all around
And and
Such a sense of joy upwelling

God be praised and thanked!

I WILL GIVE YOU ONE MORE DAY

I will give you one more day and then
And then
All the joying and lightening ripens to
    fullness
And what comes forth from you may
    never again be the same
As what it once was or what you
    thought it might be or even
Wanted it to be
None of that matters much
It will have its own life-way
And you will watch in wondering open-
    eyes and
See the very bursting forth of life in
    between and around you and
Know that
God very God true God is always
    always always

THIS MORNING

I was slow to get up this morning
Using the snooze alarm over and over
Enjoying my body in my comfy bed
Turning over and then again
Turning back, not wanting to
Leave my inner consciousness of
Half-awake dreaminess and the
Pleasure of my body
Snuggling up in my covers
Pain-free for the moment

After, I was ready to get up
To my day
Satisfied somehow.

EAGERLY WAITING

Well, here I am, wondering
What within me is waiting eagerly
Slowly longingly to come out into
The world of soft air   blossomings
Along the way and enormous
   over-stretching
Peace and immensity

In all that immensity is, somewhere,
My voice   my heart's longings
To be   to give   to share

LANGUAGE

As always
Language
Language that breaks my heart
With beauty
That opens my layers
Underneath with
Knowing of a truth
That keeps me in the stream
Of my deeper life

MERGING

Drifting in silence
Lost in the stars
I wonder
I wonder about my mind
What is mine
And what is not
Somehow there's a merge
I can't really find the boundary
Know the full truth
Can only feel my thought
My feelings
My essence

BOUNDARIES

There's a reason for fences boundaries
Individual houses:
I cannot write as well today;
Others are too much with me
In the inner world.
It makes it hard to find myself
My central core
From which my poems spring.

Alas alack oh me oh my!

LINKS?

Is everything writers write
From links with other minds?

LEARNING

Surges of excitement and others' pain
Are apprehended by me in my inner
    space.
That is, in fact, true. What does it
    teach me
About how humans are always
    connected up
With someone, known or unknown
    someone?

Are none of us really individuals or are
    we, from
Day to day, simply composites made
    of others'
Minds and feelings and thoughts,
    never simply
Ourselves alone?

Does it mean that there is really only
One Mind linking here and there,
    minute to minute at
All times with this and that?

FLYING

I can feel myself fly away inside
Not only when I am asleep
Dreaming perhaps
But awake times too
I think I don't really understand
Why this happens

Inner world
Outer world

I WENT AWAY TO A BOY

I went away to a
Boy who lived inside
With me

I don't know what he wants
Or needs today
But the pull is strong enough
To take me away from my outward
Life and into the place where
We meet and mingle

I don't know what I do for him
Give to him   provide
But I trust that God has made me
This way
Others too   everyone
And that we help
When we are called
And are also
Helped when we do the calling

COME

Guardian angel standing by
Carrying that Light in your wings
For all who need
Come be with me
Come be with me

PJ

I cannot thank you enough for the you
    that
you have been, the place you have
    lived in
with me, inside of my beingness. You
    were
one of my companions in this long
    life - you
with your strong heart for others,
    your responsible
self, your wildness, your long nights of
    music and
writing in your journals about yourself
and others you have known, your
    willingness to
explore and learn, your strong arms
    carrying many,
the songs that came from you into life
    on paper and
into others' lives through your concerts -
    all the many
interesting things you came to know
    in Appalachia:

clogging, hammered dulcimer, fiddles,
other instruments and voices of the
    woods and hills,
two-stepping and George Jones.

How I have grown into new interests
    and different
life from having you inside all these
    years as one who
prayed for me and shared yourself in
    some unknown
unbelievable way!

And I have not seen you in your body in
more than twenty-five years. What
    wonder is
this, that we can and have been close at
times and known each other
    distinctly yet
lived so far apart in the world.

SHE SAYS TO ME

It is seamless, my friend,
Our joining. We are not separate
From each other
But always connected.
We can move more into our
Particularized self or more into
Our seamed self with ease,
Without stress or tryingtoohard.
Know that this so!
This is and has been
My gift to you.
So it is with those
Who have left us here
And gone on,
Their bodies at an end.
They also can come closer in
And go farther away
With stressless ease.
We do not need to be afraid of
Losing one another.

THOUGHTS

Thoughts come and go
No fixed decision
But wandering
Fixing not on this and that
Stopping not to stay to
Hold to keep,
Coming and going
Meandering
Don't assume fixededness!

STRUGGLE

There seems to me to be
In my mind a struggle
Wanting so much to be myself
To be my own voice
And yet feeling often
Tethered bound grabbed by
Others and mingled

I see as I write that I am
Fighting who I am
Fighting the flow into and out of others
The merging coming-closeness
Blending that occurs between
Me and others

Am I just like dandelion fluff
Blown this way and that by
Someone else's beingness?

I guess I need to more fully accept
That the boundaries of individuality
That I always thought were there

And that I thought were right
Were not the truth of beingness in
Our world and that the flow in and out
Is what is more the truth of reality

SAYING HELLO

I did not know what I would write today
Of myself and not of myself but
Others' lives near me
Of my memories
I am so quiet still holding my
Body energy open

Today there seems to be no
word-poem
In me I need to stay more still more
    quiet
Waiting hoping yearning toward that
    line
That sometimes opens in me
No memories come to mind
Nothing that someone else said that
    opened me
Right up to a new place in myself

I hear the cars on the highway nearby
Feel the slow space in myself
The air fresh soft sweet gentle
Memories of the full-blooming oleander
Beside the road startling me with its

Wild magenta beauty

I go to my poetry group eager to
Write share listen to others' new-
    written words
Absorb the sweetness of the energy of
Others be part of what we do
Alone and together
I feel my own wholeness
Blossoming

I've been in the house so much I
Can't quite realize it
That I am out and about
Among people and
Breathing good plentiful sweet air
Noticing the crows calling and cawing
All around my house
Stridently
Pay attention to me, maybe they are
    saying
I say back Thank you birdies for being
    there hello birdies
Hello today and I look high in our trees
    and roofs
Looking to see them wanting
Them to know I am saying hello

I SHALL TRY

I shall try to switch my focus from
Inwardness to outwardness as the
Bells ring somewhere outside
Hear the whirring of tires on the hot
Macadam road beside our church
But I am most aware of the peace in
This room as we all are writing our
    poems

WHO WANTS ME TO

Is it wonderful
To delight in oneself
To sense the miracle of
One's own being
It doesn't feel egotistical
To me but reverent
Somehow

Acknowledging the pull
Towards certain things
And the complete disregard
For other things
Wonder always where that
Pulling comes from
Who wants me to read
Science
Who wants me to learn about
Aliens and UFOs
Who wants me to play with
Words
Who wants me to share

BETWEEN US

Between us and the Other is something
Greater and wider and softer than
Flaming suns and wild flying light
Curving and rolling along and between
And wondering where it was and is
And
And
Who am I then to behold
The wild immeasurable fire and light of
    delight and torment
Growing in my body and mind
Without my stirrings
Whispering along the nerve pathways
    of brighter light and fire and
Rejoicing
That comes always and underneath
    the beginnings

WHERE AM I ?

I think I am not so much in the world
Today as in my inwardness my
Interiority
My mind seems not to want to come
Into the place of soft sweet air
Blossomings bloomings all around
People here sitting beside me
Sharing themselves
As I try also to do
Only a part of me is here in the
Outwardness

AFTER A DREAM OF A LOST LOVED ONE

A bird song
The clear song laying on the wind
The clear sound laying on the wind
My soul flying alongside
Their sweet and beautiful
Bodies

UNFOLDING

The gradual unfolding of
A heart and mind
As two find each other and begin a
Love, grow into a love.

So many parts of you to
Come to know-
A lifetime adventure!

SUMMER NIGHT

He called the air out
On such a summer night
And
And
And
We

WE

Moon shadow quietly moves
across the sky
between the skeletal tendrils of the
    trees
The night is luminous
We breathe in
transfer it each to each
gentle eyes   quiet hands
naked I-am and you-are.

I COULD KISS

Beloved, beloved,
I guess I could kiss your hand
And then there's your littlest toe - I
Could kiss that one, too. I could
Kiss the fingernail on your littlest
Finger. Or maybe a corner of
Your shoulder on your back. I guess
There are lots of places to kiss you
And oh how I like to think about
Doing that, making you laugh,
Me kissing and you hugging.
Sounds good to me.

Oh! I forgot your elbow.
It should have a kiss, too!

And then there's the inner crook
Of your elbow, the backs of your knees,
The soles of your feet, and maybe
Every little toe and finger.
So many kisses, I must be sure
Not to miss anywhere. Hairs on

Your head and chin and
Finally, your soft and giving lips.

I'd better not talk about kissing what's
In-between!

SOFT

You make softness in me
Whenever you come close to
Love me

MY BODY

My body is lonely
And longing

LOVE-SICK

I am love-sick
Heart-torn
Little pieces of me
Disconnected from
My all

GRATEFUL

You came from there
To love me again.
I am so grateful,
Not only that you are
Able to come
But that you choose
To do so.

I MAY NEVER

I may never give again to you
In the way that just now I have done
My heart beats so strongly
Through and through
And I know that I love you
Always and forever
As Mother used to say

There is no point going away
When people we love are so dear
So dear to us

I would not ever wound you again
If I could refrain from it
Surely you know in your heart
That my desire was not to harm
But to help

YOU STAYED

He: If I gave you my mother then
You might have cried and cried
All through me

I was afraid that cascades of
Feeling might frighten you
Into running away

But you stayed

THIS MAN'S BODY

This man's body
In his clothes
Looks like your body
And I remember
I remember
With longing

THUNDERSTORMS

There was such a rush of feeling
Rising up in me
Floods thunderstorms
Great washes of movement and water
Life! Life!

I am so grateful that I have been loved
By someone kind and good
Generous and peaceful

I will never go back to who I was
Never

DO YOU STILL

Do you still laugh?
Bubbling-over merriment?
I ask.
Yes, he says emphatically.
I am so happy, then, I say.
I love your merriment, your
Fun-playing, I say to him.

HIS GRUMPINESS

His Grumpiness
Is back again.
I need to pull out
My wonder-working tools
To help him find His
Lovieness again.

Or maybe touching is
All he needs.
I'd better ask him.

Do you need touching,
Grumpiness?
Probably, he says.
Probably, (irritably)
He says.

Maybe you just need
To be left alone,
I say.
Growl, he says.
Whoops! I think.

What to do?
Touch him a bit? (Yum!)
Leave him be?
Who knows.

He touches me!
His Grumpiness has left,
His Lovieness has returned.
The End.

SILLY ME

I love you for all your silliness,
Someone says.

I am so glad,
I say.
Thank you for telling me!
I say.
And smile.

WELCOMING BODIES

Your body welcomed me
Seriously seriously huggable
Welcoming bodies make everything
All right to me

They say that touching a child
Or an animal helps them know
Instantly that they can trust you
I knew instant trust when
I met you
Even without touching
Always trusted you
Even when I was angry with you

Wanted to wrap my whole body-self
Whole complete me-ness
Right around your heart
Snuggled in to comfort and
Love you
And to be wholly loved
Comforted
Married within
I wanted to help your body
Heal itself

Heal itself and live
To give again to others
And to me
Knew you were needed in
The world

Your body welcomed me
And my body opened and
Welcomed you
Wholeheartedly
Our bodies and beingness
Welcomed each other
In joy

PRAYER-BODY

I went into your light-body with
My light-body
Wrapped my whole self around
Your heart to
Give my energy my
Love to help you
Heal
Couldn't bear to lose you
To death   Couldn't
Bear the loss to the world
Of your goodness   your
Gifted heart for others
Even your unusual skills
Couldn't bear to lose you
Gave everything in my
Body and soul and heart
To help you heal
That was my deepest
Intention
I wrapped my light-body
All around your heart
In your light-body

RE-WRITE

Dear one, he says
Re-write your life
In me and say we will
Always
Be together
Somewhere inside

Do not deny the reality of
Evermore and always   for
Life and particularity go on
Endlessly
Without surcease

Remember our
Unendingness
With joy and great
Expectation for
What will come as well as
What is now this minute
This deep moment in time

Don't forget that I told you
Reminded you of
Unending life and beingness

BODIES

Bodies are loved   bodies are
   important too
I mustn't forget this   Mustn't
   forget
Those other-people's-bodies, and
   my own
The tenderness in me for our bodies,
   each one's fingers
Hands textured hair soft warm skins
   and pale
Whiter skin   All shades of brown red
   yellow pink
Soft coral   pale ivory   And eyes
Oh eyes   And the moist inward and
   outward
Parts that fit together so joyously
   softly   tenderly together

OLD MEN'S BODIES

I like old men's bodies
Flat butt pouchy belly
Tufty white hairs from
Ears nose eyebrows
Even tufty head-hair
Thinning balding
Sprouty thick unruly
Age spots on hands arms
Face   elongated ears
Soft squishy yielding flesh
Or wiry reedy strong
I want to get close snuggly
Feels a comfy body to me

WOULD YOU LIKE

I wonder if you would like
My old woman's body
If you saw it

SPOTTED ME!

Good heavens!
I have five age spots
On my left hand
Brown spots
Five of them
None on my right hand

My goodness!
Am I that old?

A NEW BATCH PATCH THATCH

A new batch patch thatch
Of white hair is springing up
Bursting forth
Sprouting out of my head
At my forehead
I saw it today in the mirror
On the visor in my car

I felt astonished

I have had the same small amount of
    white hair
At my temples and
Down beside my cheeks
It's always been so small
Minor
Insignificant
Hardly seen

Since I am 68 and
That is all the white hair I have had
The rest nicely honey-colored and
Somewhat darker than when I was
    young

I figured it made me look a little
Distinguished
Definitely not old
Wiser?
But there has been no new growth of
White hair that I have noticed
In a long long time

I still feel astonished

Silvery white patch thatch batch
Sticking almost
Straight up
Undesigned hairdo
Free-wheeling
Doing it's own thing

Wow

It has a life of its own
Its own direction
Its own choice of change

Hmmm

I feel mostly pride that I am
Becoming a white-hair
An Elder
An Old Folk

OLD WOMAN'S VOICE

My breasts aren't up there
They are down here!
My breasts don't like being pushed in
    from the side so they
Stick out more in front!
My breasts don't like having to
Pretend they are young
In order to fit into all the
Bras of the world economy!
My breasts want to sag in peace
They want to spill over to the side
Where they belong
They don't want to be squashed flatter
To make them appear smaller
Or pushed up and in to look bigger
My breasts don't even want to look sexy
They just want to be the soft
Comforting pillows that they are
Able to comfort and cradle
They even want to swing free
Forget being pouty and pert
Chicken necks of the old suit me
    fine too

Same with flabby sagging upper arms
I am going to throw all my bras away
Until they decide to make some that
Allow MY breasts to be themselves
Low and soft

MAYBE

Maybe my hair will turn white one day
It seems to start to do it
A few strands whiter and whiter
But not the rest yet
Strange to be 76 with
Honey-colored hair

My face-lines seem about the same too
Maybe a few more or deeper
Wrinkles but nothing too
Noticeable   Are the years
Really passing and am I
Really aging
Moving toward my own end here
On my dear earth

Why am I not marked more

THE LONG WAY

Who would like to know my old-woman
    self
Of all my old dear ones
From all of my life?
Does anyone want to stay around me
As my hair turns white and
I get wrinkles and age spots on my
    skin?
As I lose parts of my memories,
Fumble for words that I can't quite find,
Let go of loved activities as my body
    becomes
Less able.
Does anyone want to continue to
    know me
Through the rest of my life?

I want to know the old-person selves
Of those I have known and loved.
I want to see them, to hug them,
To comfort and appreciate them and
Their friendship.

They knew me when I was young and
When I was middle-aged.
Now I want them to know me as I
Become an old person,
I want them to see me through until
My death and remember me with love.
I want them to go the long way
　　with me,
Let me go the whole long way with
　　them.

EMBRACE

I lie on the breast of the earth-world
In my heart-mind
Seeking to embrace it and
Let it hug me   hold me
Hang on to me
Its life and mine intertwined

Oh keep me there a while yet

IF

How would it be
If the emanation from each of us,
From all parts of the earth,
Was good will?

THESE PERFECT THINGS

Maybe it makes an enrichment in a life
To live the day-to-day
To put aside the soul's direct
    expression
And find the center of
The daily round of home friends family
    work
Bees and trees and earth's
Sweet sighing under the spring's rains
Flowering of leaf and bush and stems
And sweet fragrant smellings in the
    woodlands' openings

Oh, that I might give these perfect
    things
To my soul in all its wanderings
    through time and stars
Planets and galaxies and suns'
    streamings
Give these perfect perfect things
That I found here on the earth
A home in my soul-self

BEAUTIFUL DAY

Beautiful day, beautiful day
"Rejoice and be glad in it," my Bible
  says
And I can't help it! I do!

I COULD CHOOSE

I could choose mornings,
windblown, tossed and tousled skies,
     after rain
fresh and clean and clear.
Gray skies, pearled, before the
sun's fully up and
goldening all beneath.
Misty dampness, waifs and whispers
of fog, drifting, drifting,
before drying and clearing.
Soft fall of rain, skies gray and
cast-over the sun and moon, trees
dark against gray, and dripping
and the birds wheeling, chirruping,
busy and bright-sounding.

I could choose mornings,
instead of rising late, and
only going to sleep after midnight,
when all is still, still and quiet.
Even the birds.

TONIGHT

A misty sprinkly grey evening
Twilight-time
Trees tendrilled   skeletal
Lifting branches up into
The grey sky
Peaceful   like air and
Light after snowfall-twilight
Smells good   The slight wet
Mistyness feels just right on
My skin face hands
Did I tell you how
Beautiful it seemed to me
To be?

LIGHTS

streetlight lights
restaurant lights
business lights here and
there   I feel at home now
this minute in the grey and
quiet   as if nothing tonight is
changing bustling noisome
somehow I am enclosed in the
stillness

WHAT MESSAGE, CROWS

The crows calling this morning
Were harsh insistent
Repeating

I wondered what was wrong
What they were alerting each other
    about

Later, coming home
Found twenty or thirty crows
Moving around on the ground
On the grass   on the driveway

Usually they are in the trees

GOLDEN HILLS

The golden lion-pelt hills are gone
Brown sere are the fields grasses hills
Winter on its way as
Sleeping comes upon us
Turning us inward to hibernate
Resting fallow like all
All else in our world

TIGER

I rest my cheek against flank of
Beautiful Tiger
Feel his breathing through his whole
    body
Want to rest with him   against him
Want to forget about his savage nature
Trust in his contented motherfather self

TREES' GIFT

And the trees bow down
Bow down
Leaves rub together and sigh
Hearts' gifts
Given free
God's bounty all around
To set the spirit free
Into quietness
And depth

Miles to go
Away
Miles to stay
Nearby
White woods creep
Silently
Through the day

YEARS AND YEARS

Trees leafing greening
budding blossoming
Shedding

Am I the same
Over and over
Each year of my life?

SPRINGING

Sing! Sing!
It's spring!

The grasses are greening
Trees feathering
Some flowering blossoms
White and pink

God grant me hills and fields

STUCK

I lay my health problems before you
Oh God of tenderness and mercy
I lay them on your altar in my deeper
    mind

I want my body to heal of its pain
It's stiffness
It's damage
I'm stuck, Lord
Not knowing what else to do

I've worked with my issues
Wailed through my grief and loneliness
Prayed often for my every cell to be
    turned
To your Light

I'm stuck, Lord
Really really stuck
Please fix it!

THANK YOU

Oh Lord, thou hast searched me and
   known me.

I will not hide one small bit from you.
I am completely open to you to know.

The darkness and the light are both
   alike to thee.

Thank you for your ongoing forgiveness,
   acceptance, and love
Even without and before my asking.

STOCK MARKET PRAYERS

May the prayers of gratitude fly up
    to God
Every day every minute
For the stock markets' growth and
    steadiness
World-wide for stock markets
    everywhere
Prayers flying up from
Grateful hearts

HAVE I FAILED THEN

Have I failed then to find
That beauteous peaceful line in me
After all these years of work to
Become peaceful loving healing
In my energy field?
Have I then
After all
Failed at what I wanted to do?

Others' assumptions about me
What I was trying to do to become

Was it so hard to see and feel my truth
My choices expectations
My intense desire to have an energy field
Non-harmful welcoming accepting
Peaceful peaceful full of peace and love
Was it so hard to see me
To understand my earthly journey
To be clear about what I wanted
To become to be to express

I feel such sorrow sometimes
If I have been misperceived
That who I am did not shine forth
Clearly

PLEASE NOT YET

I don't know about other people
How they feel
But I am not ready for death
To come for me
Do we have any choice in the matter?

I expect heaven to be a loving
Place of peace and beauty
But I am not ready yet
To let go of all I am doing here

Thinking of it
I grieve feel blue
Sad pressured by time
To let go before
I am ready

I haven't finished planning so
My daughter knows what to do
With my belongings and
My poetry books in process

I want more time to listen
To music to birdies to

Kids yelling playing
Calling out outside my house
Want to read more of
My books

I think that I might end up in
Assisted living and need
Lots of books and music
Games and jigsaw puzzles
On my iPad
To fill out my years still
To come

I don't want to
Let go of everything
Yet not yet
Please

WHO ARE WE THEN

Who are we then
After the dying of
Every close friend
Parents brothers
Sisters   others who
Mattered to us   lived
Closer inside us
Than others we knew

Who are we then
When that inner field
Of consciousness changes
So much

Is there inner
Emptiness
Or does something come
Closer within us that had
Been covered over by the
Consciousness   the essence
Of friends and family

Have to wait and see
I guess
I haven't lost everyone
Yet

UNDERNEATH

In my underneath life I
Want so much to hold
People and creatures, plants
And trees, all life,
In my heart in some good
Way that makes life easier
And happier for them,
Want to hold all the earth,
In my mind, aware of inter-
Connectedness and love.

In my underneath mind,
Moving, flowing outward,
Endlessly giving as the
God-force is, may it
Go on every moment, in
All situations, with love,
Compassion and good will
For all, never having to remind
Myself again, knowing it
Will ever flow out for all
As God has made us to be.
Let there no hindrance be

In me that blocks that flow
Or turns it toward negativity.

In my underneath life,
In my underneath mind,
O Lord, let it be.

NESTLING

Not into the littlenesses of
shouldsandoughts, rightsandwrongs.
Let it free of all that,
Freely flowing,
Undendingness of Love's flowing
In and out through me, through us,

Cradled so in each other's hearts,
Curled up nestling in each other's
Bodies, arms, spirits,
Leaning in to wrap our selves
Round each other,
Whether in our minds, our inner selves
Imagining and feeling,
Or with our physical fleshness.

Such circles of love,
With the children gathered in and
Nestling,
Everyone's arms, selves, hearts
Wrapped round each other,
Like creatures in their cocoons,
Resting and changing,

Sleeping and dreaming,
All dreamy and soft.

Like plants with their tendrils
Reaching out, seeking
Otherness
Wrapping themselves around,
Trees, roots extending, reaching
    connecting with
Life in the soil,
Waters, bugs, other pieces of itself
Wrapping and reaching and
Connecting.
Ah! We are all the same in this.

I like the feel of children's
Arms wrapped round me,
Heads nestling in the soft nest of
My breasts, my bosoms, my
Soft yielding tummy,
My old body soft and yielding,
Grateful for their knowing
To curl into me.
Ah love is so.

PLEASE GOD

Oh God, let me love! Please just
Let me love
Let it flow out of me in an
Unending streaming
Unimpeded, unrestricted
To this and that
Just flowing through me and
Out of me
Going wherever it's supposed
To go
Wherever it's needed and wanted

Please, God
Let me love

DIALOGUE

I think I am through now for a time.
Another day of poeming will come
    to me,
I am sure.

And so, my friend, I have
Given again, that those who need to
    speak
In and through you may come forward
Into the light of awareness and say
    their truth,
Become more fully-fleshed in
    consciousness,
Their life in your life more firmly
    placed and
Known. Thanks be to God, that we
    can do
This wonderful thing of such
    brightness and
Truthfulness.

Pat has worked as teacher and counselor of children and adults, and as singer and actor in professional opera chorus and filmwork. She has taught Dreams and Altered States of Consciousness and has led many dreamwork and meditation workshops. She has had a full life as wife and mother.

She loves her quiet times, reading and doing jigsaw puzzles and games on her iPad, listening to many kinds of music, opening up the world through TV, sleeping and resting without time schedules. She also enjoys doing needlepoint, knitting and crocheting, cooking, and shopping.

She began spiritual journeying and writing poetry, stories and journals when she was 14, and is now a senior.

Neva Lou Kampmeier began painting in her 60s, after many years of visiting museums and art galleries. With only a child's paint set, she began, and created some Alaskan images while at one of the ferry stops in the Inside Passage of Alaska. She later studied Chinese flower painting with Phoebe Shih. She continued to paint throughout her freighter trips with her husband around the world.

Her paintings have been shown in many exhibits, as well her own show, resulting in the sale of numerous paintings and commissions for others.

Printed in the United States
By Bookmasters